NATIONAL
GEOGRAPHIC
KiDS

DOGGY DEFENDERS

TIGER
★ ★ ★

THE POLICE DOG

Lisa M. Gerry
Photographs by Lori Epstein

NATIONAL GEOGRAPHIC
WASHINGTON, D.C.

★ ★ ★

Meet TIGER!

★ ★ ★

Tiger is a **Belgian Malinois,** and he has a very important job.

Tiger is a police dog!

But Tiger is not just any police dog. He works in the capital of the United States, Washington, D.C.

This is where the president
lives and where laws are made.
Tiger works hard to keep
his city safe.

Tiger has a human
partner. She is a police
officer and her name is
Aida Rodriguez.

They help keep the capital
safe by finding things
that might hurt people.

Officer Rodriguez says, "Search!"

Then Tiger gets busy, smelling down low and up high.

Sniff, sniff, sniff!

If Tiger smells something that might be dangerous to people, he **sits** to let Officer Rodriguez know.

Great job, Tiger!

Officer Rodriguez gives him a reward: his purple squeaky toy!

Squeak, squeak!

★15★

Together, they **protect** the city every day.

Each morning, Tiger waits patiently while Officer Rodriguez gets ready.

**Tiger gets ready, too:
He even has his own badge.**

All set?
Let's go!

Tiger and Officer Rodriguez ride to work in a special police car.

Soon they arrive at the police station. Welcome, Police Dog Tiger!

At the police station,
Tiger and Officer Rodriguez
learn their jobs for the day.
Every day is different for Tiger.

Today, there is a lot to do.

First, they head to the underground railway called the Metro. Tiger rides down the escalator, then checks a Metro car.

Tiger sniffs in a trash can— pee-ew!

All clear! The Metro is safe.

Next, Officer Rodriguez and Tiger visit a school. Tiger sniffs up high ...

What a you will find if you open up your pomegranate?

... and down low.

Sometimes Tiger works with a friend. Two noses are better than one!

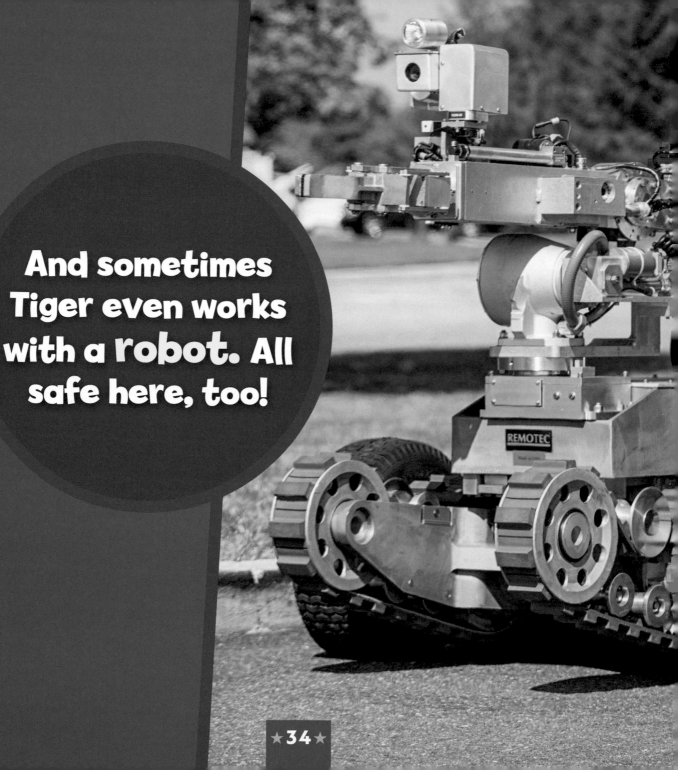

And sometimes Tiger even works with a **robot**. All safe here, too!

After a long day, all that hard work can be tiring. Officer Rodriguez and Tiger take a break.

Time for cuddles ...

... and a game of fetch!

Together, Tiger and Officer Rodriguez make a great team. The city is safe!

Good dog, Tiger! Let's go home.

Tomorrow is another busy day!

Meet the Team!

Officer Rodriguez answers questions about Tiger and being a police officer.

Q How did you get Tiger?

A The police K-9 trainers match us officers with our dog partners based on personality to make sure we get along great and work well together.

Q Who trained Tiger?

A Tiger and I trained together with expert K-9 handlers for 16 weeks. We go back to class to retrain every 4 to 6 weeks.

Q What do you and Tiger do in your free time?

A I take Tiger on long walks and runs, and we play a lot of fetch. He needs a lot of exercise!

Q **What is Tiger's favorite toy?**

A He loves his purple squeaky octopus!

Q **What is the best part of being a police officer?**

A The best part is knowing that we protect the city. It's so much fun working with Tiger that most of the time it doesn't feel like work! I put a lot of trust in him and his nose, and I know that he will alert me if there is trouble ahead.

Tiger's Safety Tips

Every day, dogs like Tiger and police officers like Officer Rodriguez work hard to protect their communities. Here are some things you can do to help keep yourself safe.

1. Memorize your home phone number and address, and the number of a guardian's cell phone.

2. Look both ways before crossing the street, and always cross at a crosswalk.

3. Make sure you ask permission before petting an unfamiliar dog—especially a working dog.

4. Never take anything from strangers, and never go anywhere with someone you don't know, even if they say it's OK.

5. Keep away from strange packages.

6. Do not play with dangerous items.

7. Know how to dial 9-1-1, and how to call emergency services in your area.

Since 1888, the National Geographic Society has funded more than 12,000 research, exploration, and preservation projects around the world. The Society receives funds from National Geographic Partners, LLC, funded in part by your purchase. A portion of the proceeds from this book supports this vital work. To learn more, visit natgeo.com/info.

NATIONAL GEOGRAPHIC and Yellow Border Design are trademarks of the National Geographic Society, used under license.

For more information, visit nationalgeographic.com, call 1-800-647-5463, or write to the following address:

National Geographic Partners
1145 17th Street N.W.
Washington, D.C. 20036-4688 U.S.A.

Visit us online at nationalgeographic.com/books
For librarians and teachers: ngchildrensbooks.org
More for kids from National Geographic:
natgeokids.com

National Geographic Kids magazine inspires children to explore their world with fun yet educational articles on animals, science, nature, and more. Using fresh story-telling and amazing photography, *Nat Geo Kids* shows kids ages 6 to 14 the fascinating truth about the world—and why they should care.
kids.nationalgeographic.com/subscribe

For information about special discounts for bulk pur-chases, please contact National Geographic Books Special Sales: specialsales@natgeo.com

For rights or permissions inquiries, please contact National Geographic Books Subsidiary Rights: bookrights@natgeo.com

Designed by Callie Broaddus

The publisher would like to thank Lisa Gerry, author; Lori Epstein, photographer; Paige Towler, project editor; Shannon Hibberd, photo editor; and Tiger, Officer Rodriguez, and the entire Metropolitan Police Department for their support and dedication to their communities.

Hardcover ISBN: 978-1-4263-3297-5
Reinforced library binding ISBN: 978-1-4263-3298-2

Printed in China
19/PPS/1